The Mind

WING CHUN

DEVELOPING LITTLE IDEAS

MATURING THEM MENTALLY
AND PHYSICALLY INTO THE
ULTIMATE MANIFESTATION OF
YOUR EVERY DAY REALITY

BY: Joseph Musse II

Author of:

Bullies – They're Not Just In Schoolyards Anymore

&

The Super Power Of Decisions – You Are Where You Are Today, Quite Frankly Because You Decided To

Preface

This book is not religious or spiritual by any stretch of the imagination; nor is this meant to substitute, negate or replace anyone's personal and transcendent beliefs – theological or philosophical alike!

This book focuses specifically on my life's journey, from the perspective of a Wing Chun artist; hence, the title of the book – *The Mind of Wing Chun*.

However, as we may 'already' know…life is multifaceted and extremely complex; involving incalculable variables. In my own personal life, I came from a position that the theistic perspective was not a position at all and was something I'd simply shrug off altogether – until a serious, thorough, methodical, objective and genuine investigative research, lead me to an entrenching study of all religions, biology, cosmology, archeology, mythology, anthropology, etymology, theology, Christology, ancient history, teleological and ontological education.

The point?

As mentioned above, this is not a religious or spiritual book. However, it would be an abhorrent and utter contemptuous disservice to my family and my own life's purpose, if I were to omit here in the preface of this book; that the nucleus, glue and omnipotent love and strength of God, is the actual and sole reason for the encapsulation of every true success in my life.

In coming to find and know God towards the former part of my life, there has been nothing my wife, kids and I have not been able to handle and conquer, in times of trouble and unsteadiness.

As a recapitulation to this preface, I'd like to be as clear as I could, so that nothing is put into or taken out of context because of any theological differences one may have regarding my faith.

The fact is this; although my personal relationship with my God and my Savior, is personally my own and permeates throughout almost every area of my life – I do not and have not ever disrespected or minimized the views and opinions of anyone else's beliefs.

It is with confidence and utter assurance in my faith that I say as I stated at the opening... *"This book focuses specifically on my life's journey, from the perspective of a Wing Chun artist; hence, the title of the book – The Mind of Wing Chun."*

My hope is that you enjoy the book, learn a few things, and store the useful and relevant aspects, cogently in forefront of your mind.

I believe it is also useful to note, that this is not another step-by-step tutorial-like book, where I walk you through cool things you can learn to do.

In short, this book, although tailored for Wing Chun students and teachers of <u>this</u> particular art – encapsulates philosophical and practical applications that can be implemented in anyone's life.

> *"What good is it for someone to gain the whole world, yet forfeit their soul?"*
> – Jesus Christ

About The Author

Sifu Joseph Musse II was born and raised in New York City, to Joseph Musse Sr. and Irma Pagan.

After living in Alphabet City, otherwise known as Lower East Side, until three years of age, he and his family moved to Tenth Street and Second Avenue. It wasn't until he was about 5 or 6 years of age, when he and his family moved on up to twenty fifth Street and Second Avenue. He has essentially lived in New York his whole life.

It wasn't until his early thirties, when Sifu Musse and his wife had their first child, that they decided to move to New Jersey!

Even after moving to New Jersey, Sifu Musse continued his profession in New York, commuting day in, day out.

Speaking of profession - Sifu Musse started his career in the mailroom of one of the largest and most successful Advertising Agency in New York [at the time].

After working his way up and out of the mailroom, he continued in the advertising arena, working at the capacity of Graphic Designer and Prepress Specialist.

Sifu Musse quickly moved from Graphic Designer, to Photoshop Retouching Specialist, to Interactive Developer. Taking his collective skillsets, now injected with a new skillset – 3D/CGI – he became the go-to-guy for all things Multimedia.

Sifu Musse learned software very quickly but was most known for applying and adding incalculable value to every agency he worked for – adding immense value and profitability everywhere he worked.

It got to the point where the roles of Supervisor, Manager, Associate Director, Director of Multimedia, Creative Director and Executive Producer, could not describe, contain or define the immense value he brought in any and every department he started, nurtured, grew and made profitable.

After becoming prosperous in his respective field, being and creating successful, fruitful, profitable and viable departments for a myriad of Ad Agencies; he finally decided to simply create his own company – Petras Digital [http://www.petrasdigital.com/].

After having an extremely successful and lucrative career, fathering three children, cultivating a relationship with his wife since they were fourteen years of age, writing two books [*The Super Power of Decisions & Bullies*] and writing this book – Sifu Musse has successfully, diligently, wholeheartedly, sacrificially, relentlessly, unapologetically, unwaveringly and tirelessly taught Underground Wing Chun for over twenty years.

Why was it so important to mention Sifu Musse's whole history here? His career? Where he grew up? His family? And so many of the other 'seemingly' unnecessary, superfluous and gratuitous information, not needed for a Wing Chun book?

It's because of the literal and practical manifestations of "*The Mind of Wing Chun*" that Sifu Musse was able to be successful in all his endeavors.

In spite of a vigorous and tremendously demanding lifestyle; attentive to very involved with his wife, kids, career, authoring, teaching and he himself still growing and learning – Sifu Musse held it all together and has become the complete embodiment and outward manifestation of the real essence of what he calls, "*The Mind of Wing Chun*"

The Mind Of Wing Chun

Acknowledging that although one may be a student, practitioner, fan or long distance admirer of Martial Arts – specifically Wing Chun; he recognizes the prevalent and more obvious dichotomy or chasm that exists in the lives of many who say they belong to an art, system or organization.

So many students, practitioners; or dare he say *"Teachers"* live a life of duplicity and never really taking in and living out the true essence and power in and of Wing Chun.

Now of course that sounds controversial. But the truth of the matter is that life is multifaceted, three-dimensional and extremely engaging. Taking any art, solely for the physical aspects of it would be to lose the scientific and internal aspects – and vice versa.

Sifu Musse believes, lives his life, and espouses the whole of Wing Chun and its application for the street, the office, the home, and in every endeavor/arena one has resolute to journey on.

With the reader and current or future student of Wing Chun in mind; Sifu Musse has set forth in his heart, to share his experiences, knowledge and wisdom on The Mind of Wing Chun, so that you too can have a much more fruitful life, living the art that you've come to know and possibly love -

fully and unabashedly, boldly and successfully – in every area of your life!

> *"It is difficult for a student to pick a good teacher, but it is more difficult for a teacher to pick a good student."*
> – Ip Man

Introduction

This book is written in a format that takes the reader through a journey of one man, who has and continues to live his life the *"Wing Chun way."*

The Mind of Wing Chun was written with the reader's life in mind. Sifu Joseph Musse is a man with a heart to help as many people as he can possibly reach.

Sifu Joseph Musse is a firm believer that one does not need to reinvent the wheel and that if even just one individual reading this book, took heed and applied The Mind of Wing Chun to his or her life – he would have achieved his goal and objective, happily and with much satisfaction.

This book was in the making for so many years, but not unlike Wing Chun, needed to be unveiled with great timing and execution.

> *"Where there is no guidance the people fall, but in abundance of counselors there is victory."*
> – King Solomon

Table of Contents

Chapter 1
Too young to appreciate

Chapter 2
Less thinking please

Chapter 3
Let's get physical

Chapter 4
Getting humbled

Chapter 5
Success through Wing Chun

Chapter 6
What about your journey?

Chapter 7
Enter your dragon – Leave a legacy

Chapter 8
Closing Thoughts

"Do not be conformed to the patterns of this world but be transformed by the renewing of your mind."
– Apostle Paul

Copyright © 2016 by Joseph Musse II, LLC. All Right Reserved.

Chapter 1
Too young to appreciate

I was my parent's first-born-son. Born January 1, 1972 – almost a full year before Grand Master Ip Man passed away.

As far back as my memory can take me; I can't remember a day when I didn't think of my father as a real life superhero.

Again, as far back as my memory would allow, my father, [Sifu] Joseph Musse Sr., was ALWAYS training! He's been "working out" his whole life and always preparing, learning, teaching and growing.

If you haven't noticed by now; my father is the one who gave me the gift of Wing Chun. Now anyone who's been fortunate enough to have learned Wing Chun knows that when I say *"gift"*, it doesn't mean I learned it through osmosis.

When I say *"gift"*, what I'm really saying is that it's a great privilege, honor and blessing for one to have his father be readily accessible and willing to teach such an incredible art – pretty much whenever I wanted.

I've been around the "Martial Arts" and "Self Defense" arena my whole life. Don't confuse my words though...by *"being around"*, I'm specifically referring to the fact that I would go and see my father training and teaching all of the time. It's not like I've been specifically learning Wing Chun my whole life. Although some might say; *"Since 5 years old? – That's practically your whole life!"*

As a matter of fact, as a very young kid, my father thought it would be best to put me in a Karate class with my older sister. He thought it would be a good idea for a kid my age to start out with Karate.

Karate classes for kids were probably the best thing for me, since I was a pretty electric kid with a touch of what parents and doctors these days are calling - ADHD. Okay, to say *"a touch of ADHD"* is an understatement but still – my father thought it would at least mellow me out and probably make me more susceptible or inclined to ultimately take serious interest and one day learn what he was doing – Wing Chun.

Well, as it turned out, Karate was not really for me. I mean... do you know how embarrassing it was for me to face my father after Karate classes with my older sister, holding halves of broken boards in her hand - which only she was able to break! Sheesh, talk about embarrassing!

Well, my father wasn't going to have any of that! His first-born-son, not being able to break boards? No way! Not on his watch.

Boy was I happy he didn't give up on me the way I gave up on myself. I believe that it was at that very moment, that my father became my Sifu. Father — he would always be.

Not only was teaching something my father enjoyed doing. Teaching his first-born-son, I believe, was his pleasure. That's speculation of course. Although there's good evidence that it's true!

Seriously though, I believe I may have been my father's most difficult student ever!

However, as the old saying goes, *"there's more than one way to skin a cat!"* Parenthetically, to all you cat and pet lovers – that's just a saying, a figure of speech - if you will. No pets were harmed during the writing of this book.

Looking back, I can see where my father started to get creative. I can see now, how he was trying to find the best way to bring me to see Martial Arts though his eyes.

So how does a grown man, a seasoned practitioner of the art, a street fighter, a student of Duncan Leung, and a father – teach a boy? Exactly as Wing Chun would have it – stick-to-itiveness, ingenuity, patience, imagination, originality, resourcefulness, creativity and an undying willingness to persevere.

My father did what any great teacher would do – he found a way.

I don't want to say that his persistence was in vain – it wasn't. However, I was just too young, too immature and too oblivious about the extreme value of **1.** A father spending quality time with his son through Martial Arts. **2.** Understanding and/or appreciating the real treasure and value of Wing Chun.

My father ended up teaching me an amalgamation of things like: Kali, Boxing, Praying Mantis, Chin Na, etc., etc. and of course – Wing Chun. Although I was learning, I was just too young, immature and juvenile to appreciate it.

Now as a grown man, with kids of my own, a Sifu to many, and a practitioner of Wing Chun – I have clearly seen the light. I've been instituting the same methodology of teaching, as my father did with me and to so many other students before and after me.

The Mind Of Wing Chun

As a teacher, a mentor, a Sifu and more importantly, a father – I can honestly say that although age is a huge factor, as to how quickly or slowly one learns –The maturity, capacity and aptitude, regardless of one's age, truly determines the amount of growth in a student, coupled with a true appreciation for the treasure he/she is being taught.

In my experience, I really don't think it matters how old or young students start their Wing Chun training. If a student is willing, ready, hungry, mature and appreciative – teach him.

> *"One can never be too young or too old to be appreciative. Once you understand, grasp, hold onto and respect that truth – real growth happens."*
> – Joseph Musse II

Chapter 2
Less thinking please

One of the most important challenges in anyone's life is the challenge of overthinking things.

We've all had a time in our lives when we've overthought something for way too long – right? Some may call this action, or lack thereof – procrastination.

Overthinking can be seen by many as a good thing. Some may even say that it's a virtue that one should harness and even grow.

Thinking is a great and inherent gift we all have. However, overthinking is, what I believe, and in my own experience, to be the worse practice of the mind.

Overthinking is the opposite and complete antithesis of thinking. Thinking is natural, calculative, objective and responsive. Thinking is the catalyst for growth, solutions, advances and real-time development through the power of thought.

The Mind Of Wing Chun

Overthinking walks the extremely fine line of doubting. As a matter of fact, I would go as far as to say that overthinking is - doubting.

If there's one thing I've learned in my journey with Wing Chun, it's that you have to take what you've learned and apply it.

When I say "*apply*", some may misconstrue my words to mean, "Go out there and pick fights!" Of course, that would be absolutely erroneous and completely incorrect.

Let's put it this way...electricity for example, can illuminate a room via the conduit of the light-switch. The same electricity can turn on the television-set in your house via the outlet on your wall, through the cord of the television.

You see... in the case of electricity, it's always on. It can power the iron, the television, the refrigerator, air-condition and anything connected to it.

Wing Chun is the electricity of the practitioner. It's always on and used for many purposes. For example: Wing Chun can be used to help protect us on the street. It can be used to help us make decisions that are a bit more direct. It can help us in taking massive steps and advances towards growth in our careers. Wing Chun can help us live a life of neutral temperament – much like Ying & Yang.

If the light switch is off in your kitchen; does that mean that there's no electricity? No, the current is always on. Wing Chun, if harnessed and utilized correctly, can work for your benefit; just as it works from the simplest to the most complicated appliance in your house.

Okay, I digress from all this analogous talk of electricity and appliances. Let's get to the real matters at hand.

Why would I take you on this ridiculous journey of electricity, conduits and every day apparatuses?

I'm glad you asked.

You see... A developed Wing Chun practitioner, learns, then applies the fundamentals and paramount rudiments of the art, through his/her every day doings.

Just as the ever present on-current of electricity travels through whatever conduit it's tasked to deliver the power to. So it is with Wing Chun in your life. One should not need to overthink how to execute or when to execute or even why execute. But rather — what to execute.

The Mind Of Wing Chun

The *"what"* command to execute, is where our output should be exerted or executed towards.

We quickly see that as we allow the principles and foundational truths of Wing Chun to permeate in and through our lives – overthinking becomes less and less effective – essentially useless.

It's worth noting and magnifying this point further, before this chapter of the book is closed. Something perhaps I should have prefaced at the top of the chapter, more prominently.

Let me tell you what I'm NOT saying.

I'm NOT saying that you need to live your life haphazardly or with reckless abandonment. I'm NOT saying that thinking should not be equated with due diligence or productive progress. I'm NOT saying that you can't apply the principles of Wing Chun into your everyday life.

On the contrary. What I am saying, is that "overthinking" can be the biggest hurdle to overcome in your own mind, rather than just doing what you already know you need to be doing.

It's very common in our lives, for all of us to "know" so much; to "analyze" to death; to "overthink" studiously, yet never even move an inch [forward], simply because you've paralyzed yourself to stagnation.

Before you start "overthinking" this chapter and its implications in your life; please consider the message.

To recapitulate...I'm not advocating a version of you, where thought is not part of the equation. Rather, I'm hoping you understand that once the Wing Chun fundamentals and proven principles have been inculcated into the very fabric of your being – overthinking becomes superfluous.

If I may be so bold, as to take the opportunity here to inject a quote from a man you may have heard of – Please allow me the honors.

> *"Don't think. Feel. It's like a finger pointing at the moon. Do not concentrate on the finger, or you will miss all of the heavenly glory."*
> – Bruce Lee

Granted, Bruce went as far as to say *"Don't think..."*, where I'm saying don't *"overthink."*

Chapter 3
Let's get physical

Let's fast forward quite a few years in my life!

Let's go to a time where I used my powers for evil. Mind you, this is not a time in my life that I'm very proud of but am writing it for your benefit.

I've already alluded (above) as to how we're now entering a phase in my life in which I'm not too proud of – so I ask that you read this chapter with a minimum amount of self-righteousness.

So here it is...

At this point of my development with martial arts, although in the grand scheme of things, I was by far "really good" with Wing Chun, Boxing, Chin Na, Praying Mantis, Kali and anything else my father had been teaching me till this point of my life – I had an insatiable urge to test my skillsets!

Now for some schools and for some teachers/Sifu, going out to fight and "test your stuff" is applauded and even implored – actually downright enforced!

Two problems: 1. My father taught me what he taught me, so that I would be able to "defend" myself, should I ever need to; not to go looking for fights. **2.** What he had taught me was dangerous and if applied with ill intensions – could be fatal.

As it turned out, I was definitely not using what my father taught me, for self-defense but rather, savagely causing havoc on the street, behind his and my family's back.

To sharpen my fighting skills further, in addition to what my father had been teaching me; I decided to start my very own "Fight Club", challenging, testing, and fighting the locals in my neighborhood.

The appetite for fighting and hurting people wrought an insatiable urge inside of me, to want to fight any and every one that I could.

Because of my age, my mindset and incorrigible desire for fighting – I had become the opposite of what Wing Chun or any martial art, for that matter, truly stands for – I became an animal.

Although I'm a huge proponent of "friendly" exchanges for the betterment and growth of any martial artist; I'm NOT for bullyism! [I wrote a book on bullies, called - *BULLIES: They're Not Just*

In Schoolyards Anymore! that you'd might want to pick up and read.

Yes, it's true... I had become a bully. Sadly, my father kept teaching everything he could, anytime he could. Oblivious to how I was misrepresenting Wing Chun, martial arts altogether, and more importantly – him.

I'm not sure how to put this in words without anyone getting the wrong idea but I'll do my best to articulate and convey the message loud and clear.

On one hand, I credit those days, those moments, those times in my life, for making me the person, the man and teacher I have become today. But not for the reasons you may think.

You see, in retrospect, I'm not actually sure if I would change anything in my past, EXCEPT for being a bully! With regards to fighting – of course.

What I'd like you to take away here is that Wing Chun or martial arts in general, did not turn me into that monster that I had become – it merely magnified the real me, the kind of person I had become.

Not unlike the example I gave in the previous chapter, regarding electricity – Wing Chun, its principles and foundational precepts are constant, yet neutral, both positive and negative simultaneously.

Me being the conduit, I had been the vessel in which Wing Chun flowed through. However, there's an ancient proverb that says, *"It's not what goes into the mouth of a person that defiles him, but what come out of his mouth, since it come from the heart."* If you're heart or intentions are impure, so will your actions.

I took a sacred art and tainted the very usage of it. "Self Defense" and "Selfish Pretense" may go well in a rhyme or poem but are horribly and diametrically opposite behaviors.

Sparring, scuffling, brawling, and practicing should be a part of your growth and development as a martial artist. One should test their skillsets in order to see what they have and what they lack. However, one must NEVER let the desire, drive, intentions or primary objective be to hurt without just cause!

As I prefaced at the start of this chapter…my hope is that you learn from my errors and understand that to whom much is given, much is required. Don't abuse or misrepresent the very art that may one day be there to serve the greater purpose of protection for you.

The Mind Of Wing Chun

Get physical. Don't get psychotic.

> *"A man strikes you, make him bleed. He makes you bleed, you break his bones. He breaks your bones, kill him. Being hit is inevitable, strike back twice as hard."*
> – Bruce Lee

Chapter 4
Getting humbled

As we continue this journey into the Mind of Wing Chun – let's fast forward a few years more, to a time when getting humbled left a bad taste in my mouth but served as a phenomenal catalyst for great success!

You know the old cliché – having a taste of your own medicine may not taste so good but it works just the same!

At this point in my life, I can honestly say that I was on top of the world. I was living in the city with my wife - no kids yet. We were both on journeying in our career paths, living life as well as one possibly could.

At this point, I already had several students and was applying The Mind of Wing Chun in every arena of my life. Professional and economic success was flourishing and exponentially moving steadily in the upward direction.

One of the main thrusts in my success was the perpetual small battles I had been wining day-in-day-out, week-by-week, month-by-month, and subsequently, year-by-year.

I had a certain stride in my walk. There was an undying energy that surrounded my every day doings.

We're talking about a time when I felt as strong as one can possibly feel – physically, mentally, emotionally, professionally, relationally and economically.

To truly understand the high I had been living in and why; I would refer you to my first book: *The Super Power Of Decisions – You Are Where You Are Today – Quite Frankly Because You Decided To*

In that book, I chronicle the behavioral patterns needed in order for one to have and enjoy a successful life!

However, since it is not the point of this chapter, I will refrain from delving into the details of how we all have the ability and capabilities to create a fruitfully successful life through the power of our words!

No, not this chapter; this chapter is about what happened to me one day in the midst of all that success and high loftiness.

Like I mentioned earlier... I had already been teaching Wing Chun to more than a several students, and was myself, still learning more and more from my father.

As fate would have it, one of my father's brother-in-the-art – a fellow student from the original Duncan Leung - Wing Chun School – reached out to my father and suggested that his student touch hands with me.

Soon after my father received the call from his fellow Wing Chun brother, he immediately reached out to let me know about the opportunity.

Naturally, me feeling invincible and riding the success train up until this very point – I gladly agreed to meet with this guy, so that we can talk, get to know each other and of course touch hands [do some Chi Sao].

Now what I did not know, prior to meeting up with him, was that he had been training in Wing Chun for many, many years; with many, many teachers and specialized, specifically in Chi Sao.

Let's fast forward to our little meeting.

First off, he was a very, very respectful individual and extremely cordial in his speech. He spent several minutes talking about his utmost respect for my father and my father's Wing Chun prowess – and how my father's reputation preceded him.

I agreed with his thorough, accurate assessment and point-by-point complementary exposition of my father.

After a little back and forth with small talk, we finally decided it would be a good time to now touch hands.

I was extremely confident and psychologically poised to get started.

Then we began.

We began with a little rolling-hands – feeling out each other's energy. My stance/horse was solid and so was his. Our energy at the moment was equal and unwavering.

He moved towards me, as to attack and I immediately got offensive! He said to me, *"relax, we're just touching hands."* I was a bit confused, since up until that point, I had always been taught offense, offense, offense.

By now my mind was on overdrive! I found myself *"overthinking"* my movements. *"Was I too high, too low, too forward, and too soft?"* My brain was racing wildly and my body followed suit.

He totally threw me off my game when he made the statement about *"...we're just touching hands!"* Any time prior to this encounter, *"touching hands"* meant something much more physical to me.

Needless to say, he quickly took advantage of my lack of certainty, as felt through the rigidity of my arms, which for him, was the right thing to do.

I was working way too hard now. I started to perspire profusely, as he knew that he had infiltrated my mind and was now moving in effortlessly and at will.

At this point, we weren't just *"touching hands."* Every time he moved in, I moved back. Although my hand reflexes were on point – I knew I was overthinking and overworking! Not to mention, that I had been doing something I had never done before and was not accustom to – moving back!

My shoulders started feeling sore, I was sweating buckets, I overexerted myself and above all – my ego was devastated!

Recognizing my fatigue and reading the distress of my body language, it's as if he took mercy on me and politely asked if I'd like to stop for now and continue another time. My pride wanted to say no but my bruised ego said *"Yeah, sure."*

I was hustled. My initial instinct to react offensively when we first began touching hands was deflected with a simple and seemingly innocent statement – *"Relax, we're just touching hands."*

I had allowed the outside voice to penetrate my conscience – my mind; as I started to overthink whether or not I was indeed being too offensive, when I should have just been relaxing, since we were just *"touching hands."*

Needless to say...we talked a bit. Knowing that I was feeling deflated, he tried consoling and comforting me, reminding me that he had been doing and specifically training his Chi Sao, for many, many years.

We shook hands and vowed to meet again for some more Chi Sao. He walked away with that same familiar pep in his step, which I once had. I walked away with my head hanging low – and not just figuratively.

What a humbling way to end the day!

As the day went by, I began to get progressively depressed and extremely disheartened about what had transpired.

The Mind Of Wing Chun

My *"winning streak"* and *"top-of-the-word"* attitude quickly vanished, as I plummeted towards a melancholy mindset.

As you'll see in the next chapter – there are ups and downs, wins and losses, highs and lows, victories and defeats – these extremes in life need to happen if growth is occur.

From this experience, came the phrase I'm always telling people; *"In life one of two or sometimes both happens to every human being – you either humble yourself or get humbled. I wise individual humbles himself, so that he doesn't have to be humbled."*

> *"True humility is not thinking less of yourself; it is thinking of yourself less"*
> – C.S. Lewis

Chapter 5
Success through Wing Chun

As we continue this journey into the Mind of Wing Chun; let's fast forward a few more years to a time when getting humbled left a bad taste in my mouth but served as a catalyst for massive learning opportunities, coupled with great success!

In the last chapter, I went into some great detail outlining the proverbial 'pedestal' we're all susceptible of putting ourselves on.

Now I won't lie to you...to me that was catastrophic! After having such a good run for so many years, in both my career and personal life - including Wing Chun; I had finally felt the internal defeat in a very profound way!

So what does a person who has a Wing Chun mindset do? You guessed it – go back to the source! Man, let me tell you! I went back to my father, just as soon as could, and told him about how embarrassed I was and how I never wanted to feel that way again.

Fortunately for me, this was no typical Sifu/student relationship; this was beyond that; this was a father and son relationship. He wasn't going to let me sulk for too long without giving me a word or two of encouragement.

I'll never forgot what he said to me – *"You didn't lose; he was just better than you that day. Plus, he just helped you find your weakness."* *"He"* being the gentleman I did Chi Sao with.

What a great lesson to apply in all of life! We don't 'necessarily' lose or win – we expose our weaknesses. How else would you know how to get strong at something if you don't first know that you're weak at it?

It's brilliantly simple! You see...we go through life, and in everything we do, trying to be perfect at something without first understanding and appreciating the value of the imperfection that helped us see what we're not.

Goals are obviously great. However, as my understanding of 'success' in any arena of my life starts to broaden... I'm finding out more and more, that yes, we should set those goals but it shouldn't minimize taking that very first baby step, towards actually obtaining them.

The Mind Of Wing Chun

Sometimes we get so caught up in the details that we end up going nowhere, for fear of going the wrong way. Part of our growth is using our God-given, innately built, common-sense-induced discretion. You don't just "take risks." You take 'calculated' risks. Calculated implies that some logic of perhaps a past experience, whether yours or someone else's, is taken into consideration, then you act on it without being paralyzed by "overthinking."

Needless to say, I acted.

Although my ego may have been the only thing that really got hurt, it was a tough pill to swallow nonetheless.

Regardless of the ego factor, I knew my father would be able to help me with tweaking and refining my skills in order to move forward, past my little quandary.

The quandary which was – how could I have been successful for so many years; doing Chi Sao with others, applying the Wing Chun mindset to my everyday life, yet struggled horribly at doing Chi Sao this time around?

Wouldn't you like to know the answer? Yes? Cool, I knew you would.

Well this isn't going to be a quick and simple answer, although 'simplicity' did play a huge role the second time around.

I want to lay out for you, if I could, a few key points as to what factors played a role in me not being successful – 'that' day.

Over confident

I came into this friendly hand-touching-encounter feeling way too confident. Too confident? Yes, too confident!

I'm a huge fan of being confident in everything you do. But not unlike Wing Chun, too high, too low, too soft, too strong, can work to your detriment. Just be confident – not too!

Overzealous

Over confidence can sometimes fall into the same synonymous bucket as being overzealous. When you're over confident, you may sometimes do things a little haphazardly, which leads to the overzealousness that ultimately produces reactive responses, as oppose to preemptive or proactive offence.

Uncertainty

The moment he made the statement, *"Relax, we're just touching hands."* I allowed those words to enter my brain, which in turn began to sink into my subconscious, creating in me a doubt, which would ultimately work against me.

You see, when he made that statement. I started to think, *"Man, maybe I misinterpreted his entry as an attack; when perhaps it could have just been friendly fire?"* Or *"Wow, maybe I shouldn't be so forward with a guy I just met through my father and should have more respect for?"* Or *"Maybe offensive isn't always the way?"*

In any case…the point is this… I allowed myself to accept that comment as truth. Once I did that and allowed it to permeate my mindset and ultimately my responses; I wasn't sure anymore how or if I should react at all. I was so full of uncertainty; I began to over complicate my every decision.

Indecision
My questioning of every decision I should or shouldn't have made at the time, ultimately became the mother of all impotencies – Indecision. Too many unacted decisions, become no decisions at all.

Overthinking
Inevitably, I fell victim to the all paralyzing, all progress-killing, murderous and life-halting venom we all know as – overthinking.

Once you're in the state of overthinking, you are no longer using your basic instinct, and most certainly have abandoned the Mind of Wing Chun.

Overexerting

Once your brain is on overdrive and your physical body starts working just as fast and hard – you're pretty much in for.

At this point, blood is rushing throughout your body, causing your heart to pump hard and fast, which trickles into all of your muscles contracting and becoming ridged - to the point of exhaustion.

Once you're at the point of exhaustion - it's a very good sign that fatigue is kicking in and that you have now *"officially"* overexerted yourself to the point of failure – or at the very least – ineffectiveness.

So there you have it…the six-ingredient-recipe for a great failure. What's awesome about this formula though, is that you don't have to succumb to it.

More importantly and probably more life changing is the simple fact that these same six ingredients can be found as the recipe to all of life's shortcomings.

"So what happened?" Glad you asked.

It was the tail end of spring when I had this humbling experience. From that point on and throughout the summer – my father and I worked out EVRY SINGLE DAY, refining, tweaking and fine tuning my Chi Sao. We obviously worked out on many things, other than Chi Sao; but Chi Sao was the bulk of it.

I had only one request or one main objective in which I had asked my father to train me on, that whole summer and it was to not move straight back or back at all, when doing Chi Sao.

At that time, I was employed in the evening shift at the company I was working for; which meant that I literally had ALL DAY to train with my father and truly fill in those gaps in my Chi Sao that I so desperately needed - if I were to advance at all.

Chi Sao was about two thirds of the exercises we worked on, since my father felt that refining the 1st, 2nd, 3rd and Wooden Dummy forms, would bring out certain attributes in my Chi Sao, which prior to then, I had not fully invoked.

I'd like to add here, that I still had many other obligations to take care of and uphold in my day-to-day-life; it wasn't just the 8 to 10 hour workouts that fatigued me! Needless to say, although I was physically exhausted, I could think of nothing else but the next day's class!

Let's fast forward to the end of summer.

I had been doing so much Chi Sao with my father, gaining so much more insight into all of Wing Chun's forms and its applications, that it literally became second nature to me. Meaning, overthinking became just thinking and just thinking became, no need to think – just doing!

I called the fellow that did Chi Sao with me earlier that summer – late spring. I basically asked if we could meet again to touch hands, if that was ok with him. He quickly and confidently obliged.

So we set a time and day to meetup again, to hopefully talk a bit, catch up and inevitably do some Chi Sao, or hand touching, if you will.

Although I was anxious to meet up again and excited to truly touch hands with him – there was a peace in me that wasn't really looking for some sort of vengeance or recompense. I was simply looking to touch hands with the one guy that indirectly became the catalyst for my growth spurt. I was just looking to have fun.

The Mind Of Wing Chun

We finally met up again. We talked for a bit but not for too long, as we both knew that each one of us were dying to touch hands.

So off we went! Our hands touched and in an instant, we both knew this time around, something had surely changed – or the very least – felt incredibly different.

Within seconds of touching hands, he unhesitantly asked, *"Have you been training this summer?"* Not to come across as cocky, arrogant or pretentious but not to lie either; I simply responded with, *"yes, a little."*

I was also cognizant that the last time we did Chi Sao; he used words to infiltrate my mind and ultimately causing me to unravel before him. So with that in mind, I didn't really want to focus on words – or anything else for that matter.

Actually, after doing Chi Sao and hours upon hours, weeks upon weeks and months upon months with my father – this felt too easy. Now I say that with full respect and the utmost veneration for my fellow Chi Sao friend and am not slighting him or diminishing his skills whatsoever! I say "easy", as in, I was having fun.

It's just that the complete opposite and more had happened this time around, where he was working very hard and trying to really get into me vigorously but for the moment, I felt like *The Matrix*.

Things felt so slow, easy, predictable and foreseeable; it was only a matter of time that he conceded that this time around, I was a different person, with different hands.

Different person with different hands indeed!

If there's anything you take away from this chapter or even this book, it's this... obstacles are inevitable and come often but we all have the ability to metamorphosize into something greater than our current state.

We need not look at every obstacle in our life as a misfortune or complete disaster. At the time of our calamities and misfortunes, it may seem hard to bear the weight, find answers or even just too downright difficult to handle – that's the time to step back or out of the mess we're in and objectively say to ourselves, *"What is it in this that I don't know but need to learn?"* and in searching and answering that question – growth surely comes.

You see, growth comes from the adversity that propels us to find answers. Knowing full and well that we all possess the answers needed to climb out of, fight out of and battle our way out of the current problems at hand.

The Mind of Wing Chun is like a parachute, which only works when used. It's always there; it was created for a purpose and a specific reason – to be used.

So how did I gain success in this particular case? Well I can tell you this...it wasn't because I'm so good and nobody even comes close to me! No, it wasn't that. It wasn't because I'm such a go-getter, that it's impossible to stop me. No, not that. Although it is a great virtue.

The Mind of Wing Chun is how I received victory that day. I say victory because victory is when you set in your mind and heart to accomplish something and then you do it.

My being victorious that day does not imply my fellow Wing Chun opponent was unsuccessful. My victory was personal and more profound than just "*winning*" against a fellow brother in the art.

I grew a hundredfold in that one summer than I had in previous years; not because I've never learned before but primarily because "*taking it to the next level*" for me, meant going back to the drawing board to reinforce my structure and foundation.

Drawing board to me was going back to the source of my initial Wing Chun knowledge – my father! This time around, I wasn't just learning for the sake of learning... I reached out to my father, my Sifu because I needed to go back to the one who knew me, my attributes, my physicality, my strengths and weaknesses, as well or in some cases, better than I knew myself.

This victory and ultimate success, was credited to the ability to humble myself, reflect inwardly and know that in my heart of hearts, the victory would be obtain, once I saw for myself that adjustments and modifications inwardly, would ultimately be where the answers were.

Yes, I can most certainly accredit the success to my father, and that wouldn't be completely wrong. However, the success is in knowing you <u>need</u> help, <u>humbling</u> yourself to <u>ask</u> for it, then spending every waking hour <u>working</u> hard at it, then <u>testing</u> it – putting it into <u>practice</u>.

You see, even if I went back to my fellow Chi Sao friend and still couldn't conquer the moment; I would have still been successful. The success is internal; its knowing that you put blood, sweat and tears and gave it your all in obtaining your goal of getting better than you were before!

The Mind Of Wing Chun

I'm always telling my students, friends, family and acquaintances; that in life, one of two things WILL happen; you either humble yourself or get humbled – sometimes both!

In this case, I was humbled and needed to humble myself to search for answers and growth.

The victory lies in the simple fact that not unlike the Mind of Wing Chun – One must come back to simplicity and abandon the complexity that mires our minds.

<u>Lessons of success in any arena of your life.</u>

1. Don't overthink or overcomplicate things.
2. Recognize when you've been checkmated and accept it as the beginning of growth.
3. Don't walk around with a defeated mindset.
4. Humble yourself and remember the source of your previous successes.
5. Go back to your humble beginnings, when learning was all you cared or looked for.
6. Learn, relearn, strengthen and fortify your foundation.
7. Jump back on the horse with a mindset of seeing how far you've grown, as appose to seeing how well you can win. <u>Growing is winning.</u>

8. Get back in the game with faith that your efforts will not go in vain.
9. Let the art speak for itself – don't add your two cents. Don't clutter your mind with outside interruptions and disturbances.
10. Always remember that success *is* the actual act of recognizing your shortcomings and putting in every effort and unwavering fiber of your being to grow from it.
11. Putting your newly developed growth into practice shouldn't be a hassle if you've truly learned from your shortcomings; it should come rather effortlessly.
12. Don't just look at the small picture, which is winning over your opponent. Look at the big picture – you've conquered something bigger – you've mastered the true source of your growth – yourself.

"The first and best victory is to conquer self."
– Plato

Chapter 6
What about your journey?

Although I don't know you personally, I know about you. How can I dare attempt to even make such a bold, general and blanketed comment like this?

Well here's one thing we have in common – we're both human. We breathe, we laugh, we cry, we hurt [physically and emotionally], we think, we ponder, we contemplate, we aspire, we hope, we wish, we feel [physically and emotionally] and know and go after what we want.

"Know and go after what we want"? Yes, from the simplest to the most complicated goals; we first know that we want "it" then go after getting "it."

"Prove it!" you say. Okay, fair enough.

Let's start with something simple.

Example:
You're hungry. Your brain starts to go through a litany of foods you may actually want to eat. In a matter of seconds, a deduction-list of all possible

foods to eat is made via your brains supercomputing power.

Based on a few variables, such as: how much money you have in your pockets, what you have in the fridge, how far or close is the nearest restaurant from you, how long would it take to get the food in your hands before you can actually start eating; you will make a decision.

The decision you made becomes the latest and greatest objective/goal, as you now go in full goal-obtainment-mode.

Regardless of the specific route that you actually ended up taking; success has been accomplished – you're now basking in the enjoyment of your success. Burger deluxe? See, all goals start the same way.

So what in the world does all of this food nonsense have to do with your journey?

Well, if you've read this far in the book, you should have already seen a pattern in my writing style. I'm a huge proponent of examples and allegories to help paint a clearer picture of the message to come.

Alright, so what's all this business of burger deluxe, hunger and journeys? Well, let's remember that I prefaced at the top of this chapter, that although I don't know you personally – I know about you.

As a fellow human being, I can honestly say that I know about you, because we all share similarities in the way we do things and how we do it; and sometimes why we do it.

Now I won't go on record saying that I know "*everything*" about you but I know all I need to know as being a fellow human is concerned.

Dictionary.com defines the word Journey like this:
1. *A traveling from one place to another, usually taking a rather long time; trip.* ***2.*** *A distance, course, or area traveled or suitable for traveling.* ***3.*** *A period of travel.* ***4.*** *Passage or progress from one stage to another.*

Let's stick to the fourth [**4**] definition for the word journey from this point forward.

The whole "*Burger Deluxe*" example I gave earlier, was simply to prove that you and I are almost exactly alike; especially in the way our thought process and decision making occurs. Of course, the purpose of this point was to help you see that we do indeed share certain inherent similarities.

Now that I got your full attention; let's talk about your journey!

Shall we?

Your journey is a personal one. As you move and progress from one phase of your life to another – are you prepared to metamorphosize from the person you are today, to the person you're transitioning to be tomorrow?

It might be a bit presumptuous of me, at this point in the book but I should state that the "*journey*" I'm referring to in this chapter is assuming you are, will be, or one day want to be, or even hope to be, a student of Wing Chun.

You see, this book is about the actual, factual and principally based applications of Wing Chun throughout and in my life.

The question posed in the chapters heading "*What about your journey?*" is a question to those who have found the beauty, simplicity, power and strength of and in Wing Chun.

This chapter is for the group that calls themselves students of the art – Wing Chun. It is also extended to those who have not yet found a Sifu or school but are so intrigued and emotionally vested with the near future hopes and prospects of ultimately becoming a student.

Your journey is going to be one of strength, courage, integrity, wisdom, virtue, bravery, valor and everything honorable.

The Mind of Wing Chun is not a backpack that you put on and take off. It's not a piece of clothing you wear or don't. It's not a belt or certificate that 'tells you' what level you're at.

The Mind of Wing Chun is exactly what the name implies – it's a mindset rooted in the ancient Chinese art of Wing Chun, which can be found in all of the forms and in the arts foundation and philosophies.

Definitely do not want to beat a dead horse. No, literally, that would be creepy — beating a dead horse, that is!

Okay, sorry for the old man humor – I couldn't resist.

Now back to the figurative "dead horse" story. I'm referring to the one where I was physically defeated in Chi Sao and deflated mentally.

It is at this point in time, where many give up. Some might even blame the system or even the Sifu. This is where the rubber meets the road along your Wing Chun developmental journey. Some may even become reclusive and dare I say – depressed.

Well I won't lie to you – with an ego as big as mine was – that was almost me!

Yes, I said "almost." I mean, come on! You didn't really think that after being a student of Wing Chun for so long, that I was going to call it quits – did you?

Do you think I was going to blame my father/my Sifu for my own shortcomings? No. Come on – blame my hero? Blame the world?

No, I did what every single person needs to do in order to truly move on, grow, mature and develop in ANY arena of their life. I took responsibility.

That's right – responsibility.

You know what I did immediately after owning my flaws? Hope you guessed it right. I went right back to the drawing board. I went back to my dad, my Sifu and told him what went down and what my goals and objectives were and told him exactly what I wanted to accomplish AND when.

My father and I got right into it; started training every day, almost all day. I say "*almost*" because there was that old *"job"* thing I still had to do. I mean, a man's gotta still work ☺

These are the same principles I teach and tell my students, all my friends and family alike… Life will surely throw in a mix bag of defeats in your life. What do you do? Crawl into a corner, in a fetal position and just stay stagnant?

Do you throw a pity party? Do you stop from growing? Do you point fingers at everyone else in hopes that by pointing outward, you can distract even your own self, from ever looking inward?

We both know that's <u>not</u> what you do. You're a soldier; a person with many virtues, a leader and were born with a warriors heart. You are in total alignment and in tune with your God-given abilities. You understand that there's more purpose and fight in you than even you can comprehend right now.

So guess what? A real student of the art is ALWAYS a student of the art. Even as you grow and mature to one day yourself be a Sifu, a teacher of the beautiful and powerful art of Wing Chun; you'll always be learning.

You see, yes, I went back to my Sifu/my dad, so that we can take things to the "next level." However, if it hadn't been for the fact that Wing

Chun ran through even my father's blood himself — he would not have had the answers I needed in order to upgrade myself — at least with regards to the art.

The Mind of Wing Chun. This is what affords us the ability to be successful in every endeavor, even in spite of setbacks. As a matter of fact... I would go on record saying, as unpleasant as it may seem at the moment — setbacks become that bump in the road that ultimately becomes the launching pad for a new perspective.

So the question now rises to the surface again, as it was in the chapters title — *What about your journey?*

Are you one of the millions who call Wing Chun your art? Are you a beginner, a seasoned practitioner or a distant admirer? Are you a side spectator who has doubts, questions and concerns about Wing Chun? Maybe you're interested but just need to know a little bit more.

Whatever category you fall in, I can tell you this — Wing Chun has more to offer than just its fighting aspect. Wing Chun has tremendous systematic, scientific, geometric and practical sides to it that fit nicely into every phase of your life.

If you are reading this book and are indeed a Wing Chun practitioner and call it your art – do you feel that you're applying it into your everyday life? Now when I say *"everyday life"* I'm of course excluding the days you have classes/training.

I'm talking about injecting The Mind of Wing Chun into your workplace, your friendships, your relationships, and your physical fitness.

In the same way you would deflect an attack in the physical sense, it's equally applicable in the business sense.

For example:
If you're an employee or subordinate to a boss, supervisor, manager, or owner of the company you work for; you would learn how to deflect certain verbal "engagements" just the same as you would in the physical realm. Stand your ground, be firm and deliver equal energy – all with the mindset of being your own man/woman.

However, we want to be careful that we don't cross the line of insubordination, rebelliousness, defiance or disobedience. We'll have to know that line. However, as a human to another fellow human, I can guarantee you this – the energy, aura, atmosphere and impression of you standing your ground in the most professional and respectful way will be felt and ultimately respected.

We have to learn that although we're individuals – we're multifaceted individuals. The point in this very important fact is this; although we're one, we may also, for example, simultaneously be fathers, sons, husbands, students, teachers, friends, mentors, employees, employers and much, much more to many.

However, The Mind of Wing Chun becomes the underlining constant being threaded throughout your whole daily experiences and obligations.

If your journey is about family, growth, peace, strength, awareness, humility, fearlessness, servitude, energy, power, mentorship, learning, teaching, loving, prosperity and multifaceted advancement – then this is the journey for you.

In closing, I'll leave you this little image for your mind.

A three pound Yorkie barks, barks and barks some more, at the one hundred and three pound Pitbull. The Yorkie instigates and further exacerbates matters by now snarling and scratching the Pitbull – while still barking.

The owner of the Yorkie says to the owner of the Pitbull, *"Man, I think my Yorkie's scaring your Pitbull."* The owner of the Pitbull replies, *"No, we had to train our dog not to squash little dogs that are all bark and no bite!"*

> *"Wing Chun teaches you what to concentrate on, whether you're here or out in the world dealing with problems. It's second nature for me now. I don't even get to the point where there's a problem"*
> – Robert Downey Jr

Chapter 7
Enter your dragon
Leave your legacy

Legacy [leg-uh-see]
anything handed down from the past, as from an ancestor or predecessor.

As you can see, *dictionary.com*'s definition is pretty close to and maybe even synonymous with another apt word – inheritance; which helps us better understand the importance, significance and massive responsibility we all have on future and subsequent generations – even if it's not what you "*think*" you signed up for in this life.

Before I get to the real meat and potatoes of this chapter; I think it is worth mentioning and even noting here, that I believe we all have a responsibility to ourselves and to the coming and future generation[s].

Now I understand that there 'may' be some people reading this book, who are either too young or too engrossed in their own lives, to be worried or even concerned about thinking of 'future' generations to come.

The Mind Of Wing Chun

Let me state right off the bat, that I'm a HUGE proponent and advocate for everyone bettering and coming to a healthier knowledge and understanding of one's self.

However, so long as we're alive – we will always, at some point, at some level, and in some way, be around people. For some, you may be parents, siblings, cousins, spouses, employees, employers, friends, acquaintances, neighbors, roll models, and mentors. For other, it may be a couple, a few or all of the above.

Point being; there's a good chance that you may actually be the one light, in somebody's dark world. You may not even know who it is. You may not even know that you're influencing them. You may not even know that they admire and even look up to you from a distance.

Whether you think you are affecting a life or not; or even consciously meaning to – you are. So long as we're alive, we'll always be a cause and even the effect, of other people's life changing decisions.

If you're a Wing Chun student or Sifu – the aforementioned couldn't ring any truer. You should understand full and well the deeper implications and responsibilities you have with a lethal yet unassuming art like Wing Chun.

So what kind of person ought we to be? What kind of people should we become? Most important question of all: What kind of person are we now?

Since I can't answer those questions for you; allow me to answer those questions for me – from my perspective, my personal path and point-of-view.

To set the tone, the importance and personal obligation we all have, in both, our personal lives and for all mankind alike; I'd like to extrapolate and give a mini exposition from a quote Jesus of Nazareth said some two thousand years ago.

> *"Everyone to whom much was given, of him much will be required, and from him to whom they entrusted much, they will demand more."*
> *– Jesus Christ*

At work, for example, you have a certain position. We all get paid, somewhat, according to the worth or value we bring to the company. Our skillsets and professional decorum are the intangible abilities that encompass our skillsets as a whole.

However, in the grand scheme of things, we don't get paid a lot of money for knowing a little and on the flip side; we most certainly do not get paid little money for knowing a lot. As a matter of fact, in most cases, your responsibilities are in direct proportion to your salary.

"So what does all this nonsense mumbo-jumbo have to do with legacy?"

Good question.

I was just trying to prime your thought process for a mindset and understanding of what it is to have a certain level of responsibility to adhere to.

I'll break this portion of my exposition into two branches: **1.** Sifu's/Teachers **2.** Students (present and future)

Let's begin with students.

Students
It should be prefaced and duly noted here, that even as Sifu's, we must always remain students of the art and of life, and not think ourselves too lofty for continual learning. However, I'm using the word *'student'* here to denote an individual that is 'currently' under the tutelage and guidance of a Sifu/Teacher in the art of Wing Chun - specifically.

Let's learn together, a little bit more about you. What are you goals and prospects? What is it that you would love to learn and extrapolate from Wing Chun? Do you want to one day yourself be a Sifu/Teacher? Do you envision yourself teaching ten, twenty, a hundred, a thousand students in your journey?

Are you looking to one day be a disciple, a devoted pupil to your Sifu/Teacher? Do you recognize your shortcomings, weaknesses, limitations and flaws?

Are you combative, confrontational, antagonistic or quarrelsome? Do you get along with people? Do people get along with you? Are you flexible, malleable, pliable, or teachable?

Of course, knowing to be honest with yourself is probably the very first place to go in order to help answer any of the aforementioned questions.

I mean, if you can't look in the proverbial and/or literal mirror and self-reflect, contemplate, or cogitate over who you really are now and who you'd like to become in this journey we call *"Life"* – who else is going to place that mirror in front of you?

So the first thing a good student should have is a sense of who they are, where they'd like to go and a plan of how they will get there.

Now that you have that all figured out and are ready to truly and exponentially grow to levels unimagined. If you do not currently have a Sifu/Teacher and are lost as to how to even find one – a good one at that - the next question should be – Where can I find a Sifu/Teacher that would not only teach me the art of Wing Chun, but would also be a mentor of some sorts and a true and living example of how The Mind of Wing Chun can be applied into my everyday life.

As a student, your growth is primarily predicated on two things:

1. That you have the amount of humility and fervor for the art and your learnings; coupled with the utmost respect in knowing that your Sifu/Teacher has the ability and patient fortitude to see you through the rough and tough times (which you will most certainly encounter in your life).

2. That you find or have a Sifu/Teacher that humbles himself to teach with a heart of servitude and a mind of developmental growth in perpetuity for you. A Sifu/Teacher isn't and most certainly shouldn't be one who does not practice what he preaches. If his best interest is for you to grow, learn and develop – he would have that same mindset about himself - first.

Sifu's/Teachers

At this point of the game, I'm sure that you understand the massive responsibility we have as teachers — teaching an art as dangerous, powerful, dynamic and sacred - like Wing Chun.

Being a Sifu doesn't mean you're impervious to the woes and mishaps of the world. As a matter of fact, how you handle and comport yourself in times of calamity, misfortune, distress, adversity, hardship and lack is when your students really get to see Wing Chun in "action."

It may not have been the role you signed up for but regardless of what you "think" you signed up for and what you "actually" signed up – you're in a position of influence.

You see, I've seen a lot of coaches, teachers and even parents in my lifetime, who have been in the position to lead by example, yet lacked the discipline and/or mental fortitude to practice what they preach.

Now don't get me wrong here... I definitely don't want to come across as some sort of self-righteous, nose-in-the-air, pious hypocrite.

The Mind Of Wing Chun

Everyone goes through hard times and most of us are susceptible to moments and times of solitude. Obviously, everyone has the right to rethink, rejuvenate, refresh, recharge and reappear back on the scene called life.

However, through-and-through, as a Sifu, although just as human as any – how we react, bounce back and reappear on the scene, after adversity, is how others will assess and value us.

We have to care for our students, see them through their hardships, counsel them, and be firm, fair and devoted. We have to be examples to them, as leaders, mentors and most of all – Sifu's.

I've been invited to other martial arts schools, where I see the 'teacher' sit in the corner [literally sitting – not figuratively], then tell his highest ranking student to tell the others what they should do.

I've seen 'teachers' from other martial arts schools beat the living snot out of their students, while "teaching" a drill, so that he can intimidate the student[s] into complete fearful submission.

Now don't get me wrong, maybe some students like to learn that way. However, if the student doesn't learn how to honor, respect and have a healthy reverent outlook on his Sifu, but rather, is in total fear of him – he will never truly be learning – he will be too scared to ever ask meaningful and evocative questions.

Remember, you're a Sifu, not a despot. Train hard, work out vigorously, bleed some, sweat profusely and give 100% until the days class is over!

Train hard with your students; your student will learn how to train hard with their future students. Show mercy, respect and fairness, and your students will pass the tradition down to their students.

Warning:
Whatever you do, if you're a smoker, don't tell your students they need to stop smoking. You're a drinker; don't tell your students they need to stop drinking. You have a filthy, derogatory, explicit and contemptuous mouth? Well – you see where I'm going.

Why do I say all of this? Why does it sound like I'm being so hard on you Sifu's? Who am I to espouse such inelastic questions and commentaries? *"What kind of inflexible standards are you trying to create?"* You may ask.

The Mind Of Wing Chun

Listen, the best we can do, is the best we can do. I understand that. I know it's hard. But let's not think with our emotions right now. Let's take just a little step back and away for a minute. Let's be reasonable and objective about what's really being said here.

Would you put a loaded gun into the hands of a child? Would you give your teenage nephew or son alcohol then have him drive? Would you tell your friend or family member to light a match in a room full of gasoline? If you were a bus driver, with over a hundred passenger's safety in your hands – would you drive recklessly?

If you're truly a Sifu, the answers to all of these hypotheticals, is a resounding – NO!

So now that we can agree with that answer – I hope. The question is this… would you yourself do these things?

Obviously, if you cared about the lives of others; logic follows that you would obviously care about your very own life – logically speaking.

So what in the world am I saying? Does this mean that we have to be this Goodie Tushu? Always perfect? Never doing anything wrong?

No. It just means that we have to understand the profundity and magnitude of our actions and interactions with our students. We have to be examples for what we would like them to become. We don't want to have them "become" us. We want them to become a better us. We work hard and tirelessly so that in us, they can see examples of what one day, they could become and more.

We have to set the proverbial bar really high for ourselves first, before expecting our students to soar to the same ones we didn't.

I want to be transparent here and try not to come across as pretentious or self-glorifying. I can assure you that the quick story I'm about to share, is for the sole sake of posterity, rather than popularity.

In the last several years, I've had a particular back ailment that comes and goes every few months or so – randomly whenever. I could be 100% fine for several months; still do my crazy physical workouts. I would teach and move as if I were 18 years old. I would feel strong and full of unearthly power!

However, when stricken with this random, unruly and unavoidable back pain; it is almost as if a thousand volts of electricity is piercing through

The Mind Of Wing Chun

my lower back, just left of the spine, and quite literally – paralyze me! My upper torso would concave inward towards one direction, as my lower back would balloon to a size of a grapefruit and I would essentially be a walking letter C.

In any case; now that you have that image in your mind – imagine one day which was a "class" day. Meaning, it was a day I was to teach. During the day, I was just fine but started to feel my back hurting more and more, stronger and exponentially worse!

By the time evening had come, I was in excruciating pain and shriveled up to one side. However, it was too late to cancel class, as I knew my student, as usual, were ready to rumble.

I walked into class, as all of my students literally ran up to me, asking, *"What happened? Are you okay Sifu?"* I didn't want them to worry about me or be distracted with my physical dilemma, so I proceeded to teach, like normal – well, almost normal.

We trained like usual, for almost three hours. I had moments where I was working purely on adrenaline. There were moments of absolute pain, as I would grimness with every pounding to the ground. There were moments where my students were wincing every time I would explain a drill or exposit how it needed to be done, as I hobbled feebly.

Needless to say...every time I've worked out in that condition; the following day was an even worse living nightmare! However, unlike the martial arts instructors from those other schools that I alluded to earlier – I refuse to have hungry and ready students come into my class, and me not teach!

So where does this leave you, your journey, your legacy and entering your dragon?

Well I'm hoping that you first understand that teaching is a huge responsibility. Teaching is actually a gift that you either have or don't have.

Some guys go into any 'respective' art, just to become Sifu's, teachers. If you're reading this chapter and you're already a Sifu; I would challenge you to reexamine yourself, your motives, and your life "as a whole" and ask the question that only you can answer – why do I teach?

After asking yourself that question, I would dare [as I have] ask your students individually and privately – do you see me as a man of integrity? No, I didn't say *"Sifu"*, I said *"man."*

Remember what I said earlier, whether you like it or not, the moment you said yes to teaching, that's also the moment that you've signed an intangible contract with yourself, that certifies you as mentor, teacher, role model and man of integrity. Students and others outside but close enough to your circle, will be on watch.

If you're a fulltime teacher – meaning this is how you earn a living; try to apply The Mind of Wing Chun in other areas of your life, simply so that you can see the applications and simple truths of Wing Chun, working in all facets of your life.

If you're a Sifu but do not teach fulltime – I would say the same thing – apply the principles and applications of Wing Chun into every arena of your life. We didn't come into Wing Chun to fail, to be unsuccessful, or worse – come out shoddier than when we came in. No, we persevered.

I like to say to my students and many people in general that I speak with – there's really only one word that captures the essence of any true success – discipline.

We're created to be good at, become whatever, and achieve immensely, in ANYTHING. But we have to be disciplined.

Be disciplined with your health, with your goals, with your career, with your mouth – what you say and how you say it. Also, be disciplined with what you eat and drink. Be disciplined in your relationships and in all your endeavors.

Always be a student, so that you will always be learning. In always learning, you'll always know more. In knowing more, you'll be better equipped to have answers. In having answers, you'll be in better position to teach – so that you can learn what your students need to know.

Entering your dragon
Why in the world would I write *"Entering your dragon"* as the sub text to this chapters title?

I'm glad you asked.

By now, we all know and understand that had it not been for the propagation and popularization of Wing Chun in the West; by none other than a very famous student of Ip Man – Bruce Lee. Wing Chun may have never been known, at least to us, as it is now.

Bruce did something amazing! He lived, breathed, bled, hurt and got hurt to reach, what we would say, as the pinnacle and true manifestation of The Mind of Wing Chun. He wanted a better, stronger physique – he worked feverishly to attain it. He wanted to be faster, more responsive and insanely accurate – he spent his life doing so.

He used the Mind of Wing Chun for his personal, physical success, his career success and ultimately the success we should all dare achieve – the success of legacy – he entered the dragon!

If you were to pass away tonight and your funeral was held this weekend – who would go? What would the atmosphere feel like? What would be the tenor and mood of the people who came to see you?

Just for now, let's not even go into the pain and hurt your family would be feeling.

How would your students be feeling? What kind of a loss would this be for them? What would they say and how would they respond if family members or a friend of yours stopped to introduce themselves, then ask, "*How did you know the deceased? What was your relation to him?*" How would they respond?

Would your students say something like "*Sifu was an awesome practitioner of the art of Wing Chun and almost never missed a class.*" Or "*I worked out with him for so many years; I just can't believe this happened!*" Or "*Sifu was a man of integrity, a man who showed me more out of life than just how to fight. Sifu was compassionate, a man who went above and beyond; a pillar to society and one of mankind's hidden treasures. Sifu gave me advice many times, with a real fervor and genuine heart to help see me through. Sifu taught me what it's really like to push through, clamp down and persevere with my short and long term goals. In class, if I put in 100%, Sifu put 200%."*

I mean, I can take this in so many directions but I believe that you're already getting my point. Yes, you're a Sifu, but you're more than just that. Be the very person you'd hope would be eulogized one day, with the integrity, dignity and respect you lived your life with. This way, your regrets and unmaterialized goals won't have to get buried with you.

> *"Knowledge will give you power, but character respect."*
> – Bruce Lee

Chapter 8
Closing thoughts

So here we are... finishing up our mini side journey together.

This book wasn't birthed like the Chum Kiu [Second Form] or Biu Ji [Third Form], or Muk Yan Jong [The Wooden Dummy] and so on.

No, this book is rooted in humble beginnings. This book was once just an idea – a small one.

Yea, you guessed it. This book is the product of a lifelong inculcation and foundationally based principles that I go back to every single day. This book was formed from a seed that started as small as a little idea – a thought.

Very much like Siu Nim Tau - Wing Chun's First Form – the structurally sound fundamentals, coupled with the body and mind – this book became the tangible manifestation of what was once an intangible little idea.

If it hasn't been painfully noticeable to you already - I'm not a prolific writer. My 'profession' is not in writing. I may have even missed a few punctuations and misspelled some words here and there, throughout the book. I'm fine with that – I didn't write this book to win awards, trophies or to get any accolades from anyone.

No, this book was written with the pure intention of supplying you, the reader, with a glimpse of what having an awesome art like Wing Chun in my life, has been like.

I set out to prove that you don't have to live a life of duplicity. You don't just have to be successful in some parts of your life but not others. The same Mind of Wing Chun used to excel your growth in class, is the same Mind that's used to excel in every other facet of your life.

I wrote this book because too many people just don't know that through Wing Chun, you don't have to just be good in the physical aspects of the art, although that's awesome in itself, but that the Mind is the one thing that you get to take with you everywhere outside of class too.

I truly hoped you learned something and at the very least, saw a different perspective, though different eyes.

Now you know that it's ok to strive to give it your all and really be great in the gym [class]. However, within the 24 hour period that we all have, most of our life is not spent training. But now we know how to integrate Wing Chun in all those other hours in the day that we're not training. To me, that's the Mind of Wing Chun.

Go out there and start seeing and testing all of the other potential that is out there waiting to be conquered by you!

> *"I've come to believe that all my past failure and frustrations were actually laying the foundation for the understandings that have created the new level of living I now enjoy."*
> – Tony Robbins

THE SUPER POWER OF DECISIONS

You are where you are today, quite frankly because you decided to

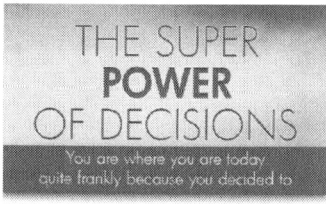

JOSEPHMUSSE II

If you've ever wondered, even if only for a moment, why others succeed in life, while things just don't come as seemingly easy for you. This book will immediately help you understand how the only one that's ever held you back towards obtaining "the good life" is you.

The decisions we've made, we make and continue making in our lives are the only reason[s] you're not where you want to be and very simply, why you are where you are this very day.

This book will show you how we're all born with a power deep in our DNA that helps us rise above any and all of life's challenges. The good news is that we were created with this power and simply need to recognize, activate and apply it in our lives.

Forget about your past mistakes, your past failures and past disappointments. Use the power you currently have at your disposal and decide the life you're going to live.

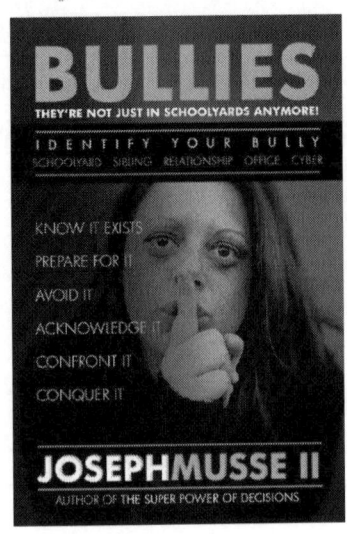

Violence seems to be increasingly growing, rising and intensifying throughout the world today. Although it may be argued that violence has always existed in the same way, with the same fervor and seemingly lack of human concern. We can all agree that since the advent of radio, television and now the internet; hearing, seeing, feeling and being affected by the violence that seems to be as pervasive and ubiquitous as the very air we breathe, has truly reached an incredibly dangerous and all-time high.

After reading this book, you'll come to see, recognize, know and understand that bullies have not only been around for a long time – they've adapted to all sorts of new breeds. Bullyism can sometimes be so subtle, elusive and mysteriously understated, one may not even know to categorize it as such.

However, in this book, you'll get a glimpse of some of the most popular bully-isms affecting our everyday lives. Whether you're a bully, ex-bully, a parent of a bully, a parent of a child being bullied, a witness of someone being bullied or you yourself a victim of bullyism; you're going to enjoy this book, the practical advice and easy-to-read language in which each chapter explains the different categories of bullies we've all heard about to some degree in our lives.

If you know someone being bullied or you yourself are being bullied, as defined by the author's classifications, you're going to love how you can handle a bully and in turn use that success to overcome everything else in your everyday life.

Joseph Musse II, Author of The Super Power of Decisions, doesn't complicate words and has a unique way to make a complicated subject – not so complicated. As an entrepreneur, martial arts instructor, business owner, artist, father, husband and lover of life, Joseph has found a way to include all facets of his life to enrich the people in his life and his hopes are that he would affect yours too.

Contact Me

Instagram:
https://www.instagram.com/wingchunscience

FaceBook:
https://www.facebook.com/wingchunscience

Twitter:
https://twitter.com/JosephMussell

Email:
jmusse@wingchunscience.com

Student Testimonials

"Sifu changed my life. I was a lost teenager when I met him, but through his guidance and instruction, I developed confidence and renewing of my mind that gave me the foundation to propel my life forward for the better, into a successful career, relationship, and overall beneficial way of living. He is not just a teacher but truly a father figure in my life. Sifu Musse is not your cookie-cutter teacher but rather gives his heart and soul into developing his students to the point where they grow immensely and transcend the teacher-student relationship to that of friend and family. He does not force his students to learn in "his" way but will instead adapt his teaching style to accommodate and best serve the individual way each student learns."

– Dom

"Sifu's teaching style is above all, for me, patient and encouraging. No matter how discouraged or flustered I get in class or out of class with my progress; he is always there to show me how far I have come and how much I actually understand about Wing Chun. This coupled with the shear brutality of his skill, keeps me begging for more of his knowledge."
– Matthew

"I've been a student of Sifu Joseph Musse II for 6 years now; and the way he teaches his students is completely honorable and transparent - never sugarcoating what the world's mean-side could look like. Whether new to martial arts or beginner to Wing Chun or advanced...he takes his students and trains them at the highest level. He then tailors the individual students learning ability, making them aware of their strengths and weaknesses. Through scenarios, he helps build an environmentally-aware mindset. The one thing Sifu Musse is unique and is top-tier at, is his teaching ability to recognize that Wing Chun does not have to be treated or used for self-defense only but in his own personal experience and books he has written, you can use Wing Chun for

business relationships and your overall daily life - Creating confident warriors on and off the street."
— Toren

"Sifu has a very good way of teaching, speaks clear with his explanations and is very easy to understand."
— George

"Sifu epitomizes the old saying that what the mind believes, the body can achieve. Sifu is extremely knowledgeable."
— Ralph

"Sifu is an excellent teacher of Wing Chun and life. He is very detailed and articulate in explaining, not only the movement, but the quality of the movement. He is also very masterful in using imagery, allegories and story scenarios to explain and/or reinforce difficult and/or challenging concepts."
— Sam

"Sifu has excellent teaching skills. He explains and demonstrates every move himself so that we can understand the logic behind the drills and moves."
— Yancy

"Sifu Joe's mastery of Wing Chun goes beyond simple movements and drills. His instruction combines science, logic, philosophy and morality into a gift he gives his students that they can keep beyond martial arts. He understands that to teach any discipline is to teach people to be human, humble and gracious. He defends Wing Chun and its practicality every step of the way - a key component to his teaching strategy."
– Greg

"Sifu has excellent communication with the ability to break down movement to a science for a better understanding, allowing us to relate everything back to the first form."
– Elliot

BONUS - Daily Exercises

HORSE SQUAT

FINGER L-SEAT

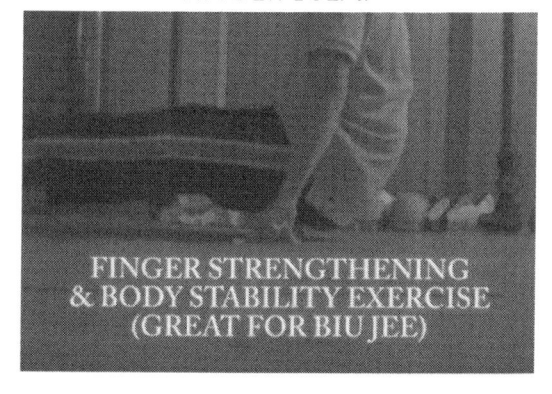

FINGER STRENGTHENING
& BODY STABILITY EXERCISE
(GREAT FOR BIU JEE)

STICK-UPS

ONE LEGGED DUMBBELL BALANCE

FINGER PLANCH

BASKETBALL FIST PUSHUPS

Copyright © 2016 by Joseph Musse II, LLC. All Right Reserved.

The Mind Of Wing Chun

Made in the USA
Lexington, KY
19 March 2017